Trace and write the color word. C[olor the] pictures.

red

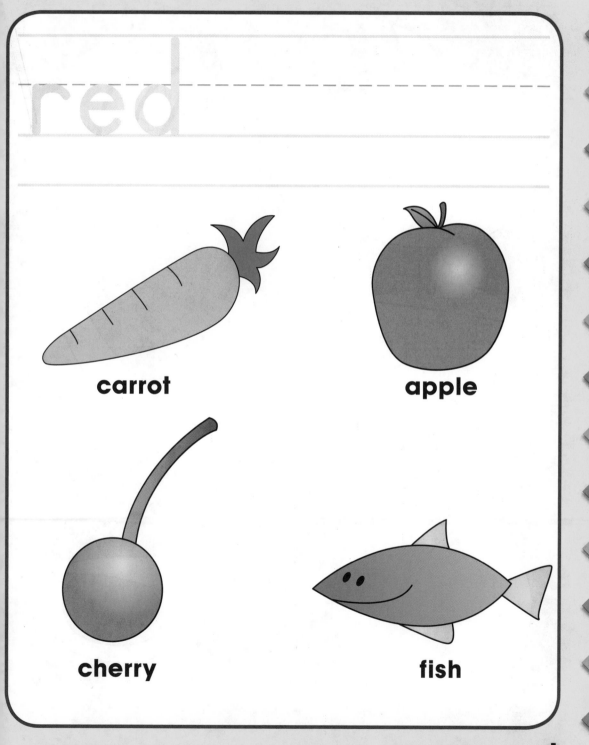

carrot

apple

cherry

fish

Which objects are usually red? Color those objects red.

CD-104334

Trace and write the color word. Circle the blue pictures.

blue

fish

blue jeans

blue jay

bear

Which objects are usually blue? Color those objects blue.

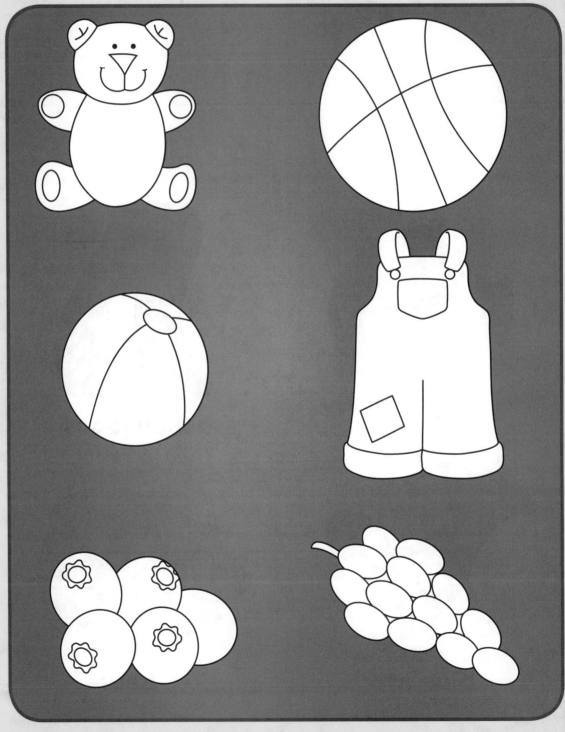

CD-104334

Color the blue jays blue.

CD-104334 **5**

Color each space to find the hidden picture.
□ = blue   ○ = red

CD-104334   © Carson-Dellosa

Trace and write the color word. Circle the yellow pictures.

yellow

bowl

banana

sun

ball

CD-104334

Which objects are usually yellow? Color those objects yellow.

CD-104334

Cut out each flower. Paste it on the circle with the matching color word.

blue

red

yellow

cut

CD-104334

9

Trace and write the color word. Circle the green pictures.

green

frog

grass

umbrella

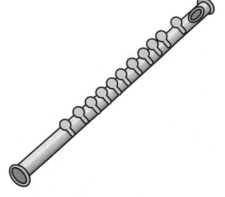

flute

CD-104334

11

Which objects are usually green? Color those objects green.

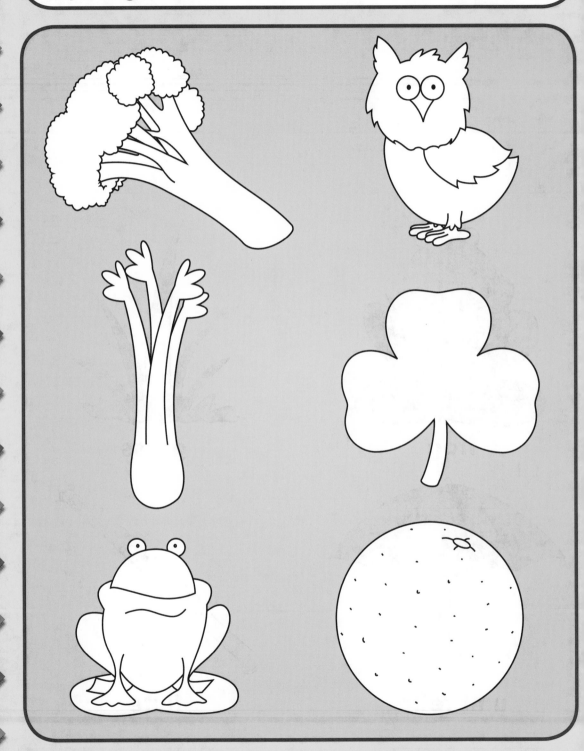

CD-104334 © Carson-Dellosa

Cut out each mitten. Paste it beside the mitten that is the same color.

cut

Write the color of each object on the line. Choose color words from the word bank.

Word Bank
green   blue   red   yellow

Trace and write the color word. Circle the orange pictures.

orange

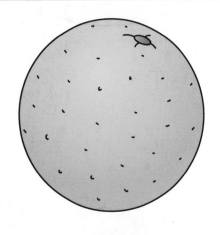

orange

apple

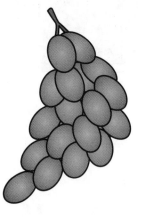

grapes

basketball

CD-104334 © Carson-Dellosa

Which objects are usually orange? Color those objects orange.

Write the color of each object to solve the crossword puzzle. Choose color words from the word bank.

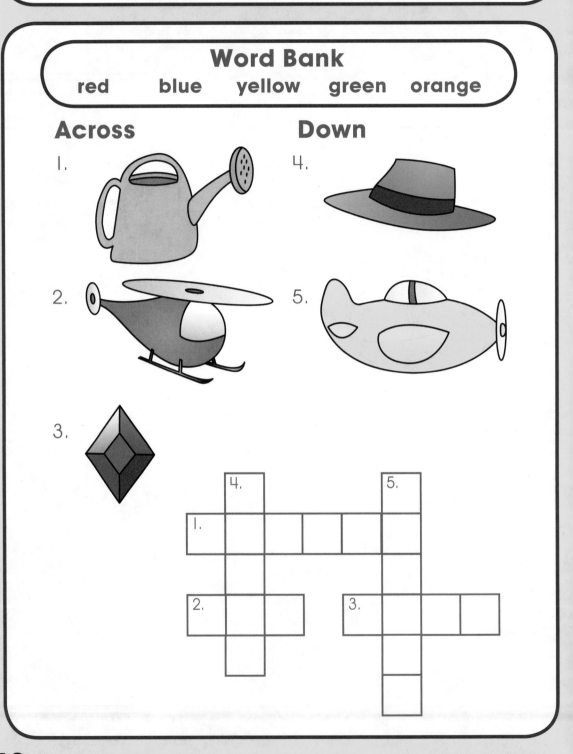

Word Bank

red   blue   yellow   green   orange

Across

1.

2.

3.

Down

4.

5.

Color the butterfly.

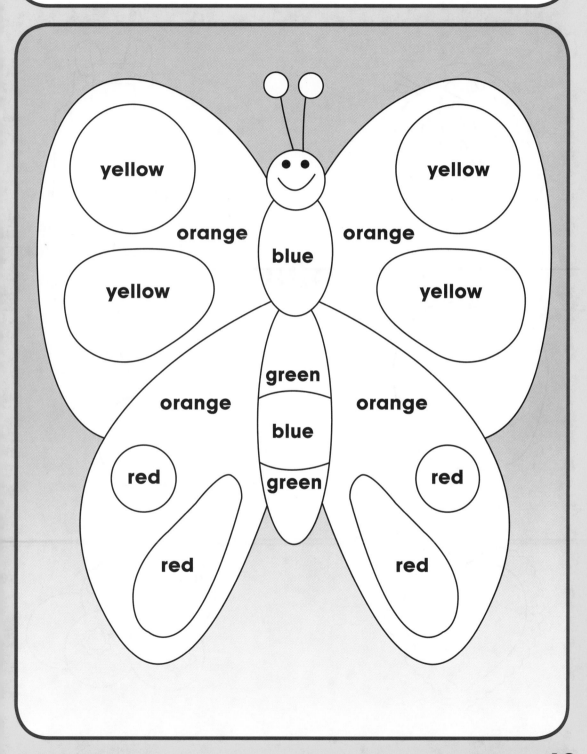

Color the objects. Draw a line to match each object to the correct color word.

blue

red

CD-104334

Trace and write the color word. Circle the purple pictures.

purple

grapes

pumpkin

snowman

violets

CD-104334

21

Which objects are usually purple? Color those objects purple.

CD-I04334 © Carson-Dellosa

Draw a line from each fruit to the anthill that has the same color flag.

Trace and write the color word. Circle the brown pictures.

brown

teddy bear

pretzel

carrot

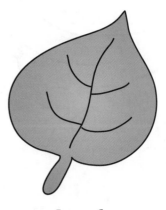

leaf

CD-104334

Which objects are usually brown? Color those objects brown.

Color the crayons to match the color words.

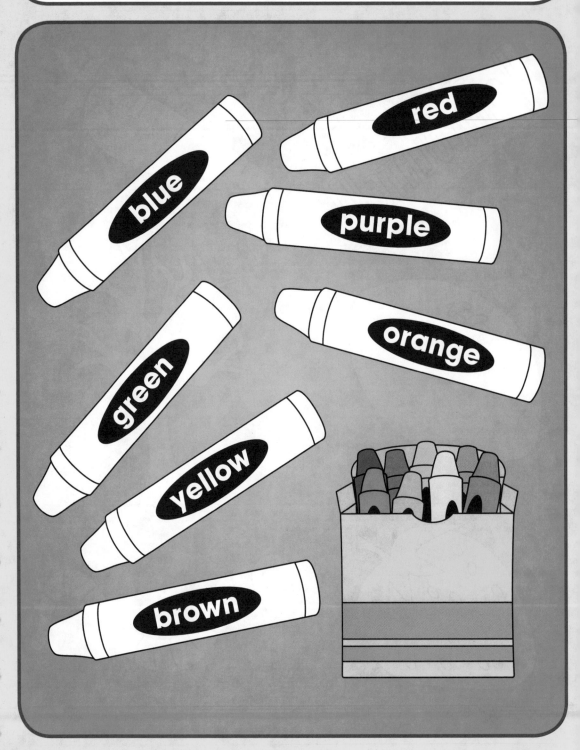

CD-104334 © Carson-Dellosa

Trace and write the color word. Circle the black pictures.

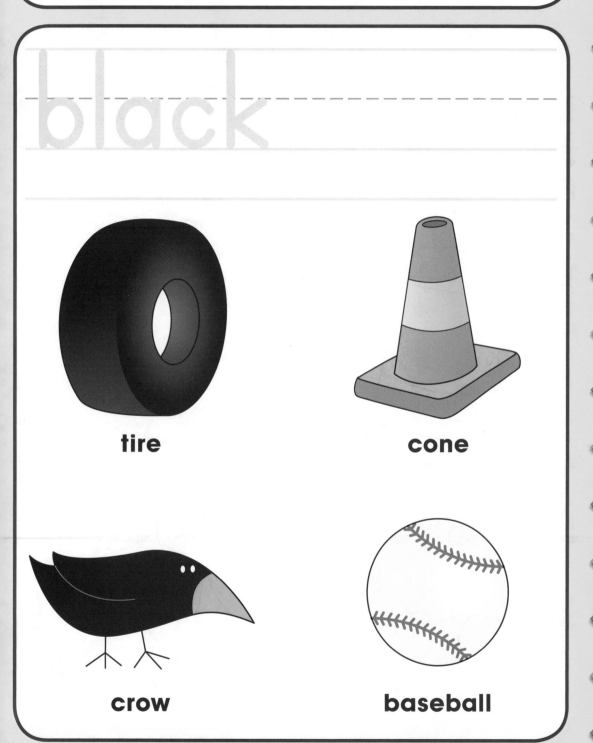

black

tire

cone

crow

baseball

Which objects are usually black? Color those objects black.

28   CD-104334   © Carson-Dellosa

Write the color of each object on the line. Choose color words from the word bank.

Word Bank

brown   orange   purple   black

CD-104334

29

Trace and write the color word. Circle the white pictures.

white

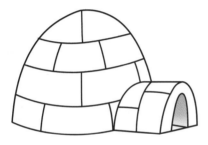

igloo

tomato

snowman

crow

CD-104334

Circle the objects that are usually white.

CD-104334

31

Circle the animals that are black and white.

CD-104334

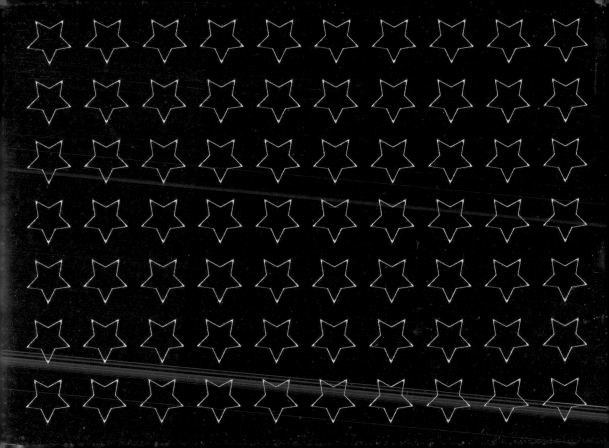

Trace and write the color word. Circle the pink pictures.

owl

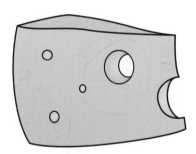

cheese

bubble gum

flamingo

CD-104334 **33**

Which objects are usually pink? Color those objects pink.

CD-104334

Write the color of each object on the line. Choose color words from the word bank.

Word Bank
green   pink   red   white

Circle the color words hidden in the puzzle. Words can be found across and down.

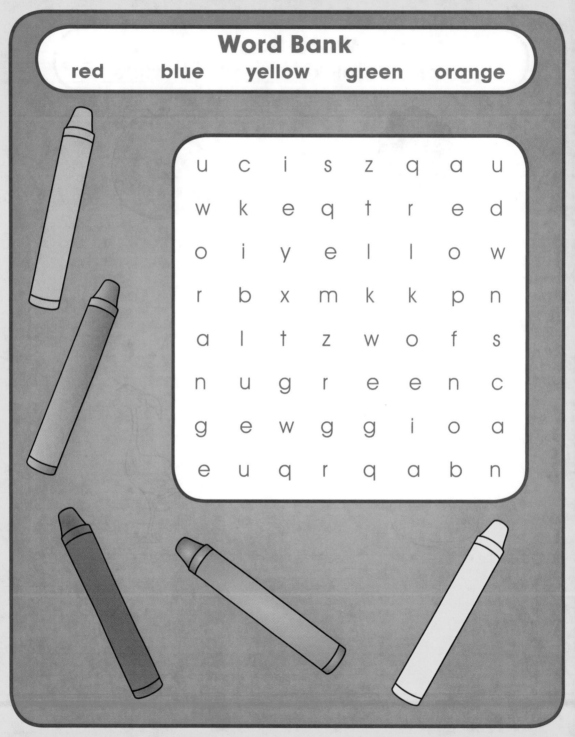

Word Bank

red   **blue**   **yellow**   **green**   **orange**

u	c	i	s	z	q	a	u
w	k	e	q	t	r	e	d
o	i	y	e	l	l	o	w
r	b	x	m	k	k	p	n
a	l	t	z	w	o	f	s
n	u	g	r	e	e	n	c
g	e	w	g	g	i	o	a
e	u	q	r	q	a	b	n

CD-104334

Color the objects. Draw a line to match each object to the correct color word.

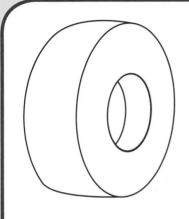

black

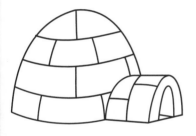

white

pink

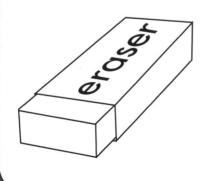

 CD-104334 **37**

Color each space to find the hidden picture.
1 = red 2 = pink 3 = yellow 4 = blue

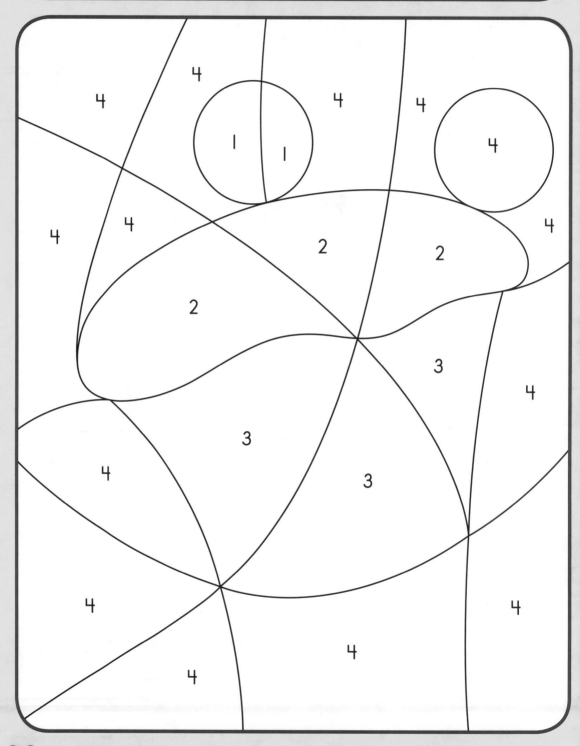

CD-104334
© Carson-Dellosa

Write the color of each object to solve the crossword puzzle. Choose color words from the word bank.

Word Bank
purple   brown   black   white   pink

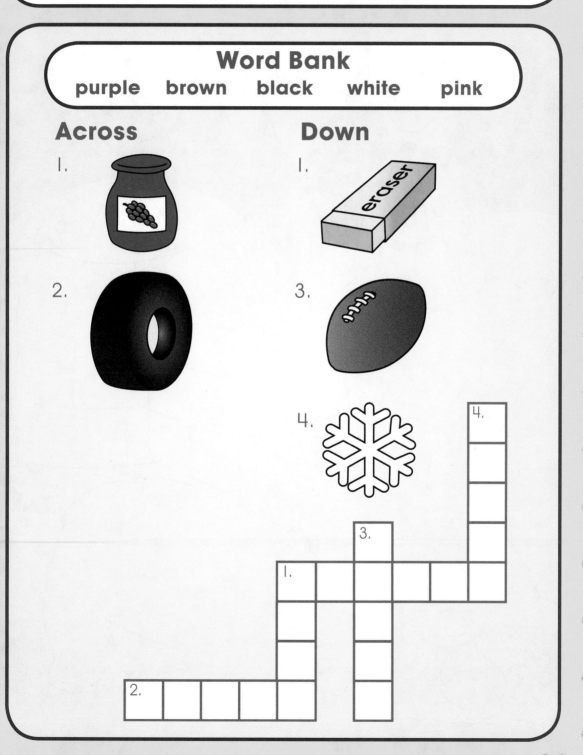

Across

1.

2.

Down

1.

3.

4.

Circle all of the snowflakes hidden in the picture.

CD-104334

Color each shape. Cut out each shape. Paste it on the shape that is the same.

cut

blue

purple

black

CD-104334

41

Draw a line through the red objects to help Beth find her valentine.

CD-104334 **43**

Color the teddy bears brown.

CD-104334

Circle the color words hidden in the puzzle. Words can be found across and down.

Word Bank

purple   brown   black   white   pink

y	m	k	m	z	x	t	t
y	w	h	i	t	e	c	b
b	p	u	r	p	l	e	r
l	i	j	p	k	x	g	o
a	g	v	i	l	g	p	w
c	t	g	n	v	s	o	n
k	x	l	k	f	p	r	y
b	u	k	q	w	p	m	w

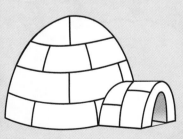

CD-104334

45

Color the pumpkins orange.

CD-104334

Draw a line through the brown objects to help Maria find her pretzel.

Color the eggplants purple.

CD-104334

Cut out each shape. Paste it on the shape with the matching color word.

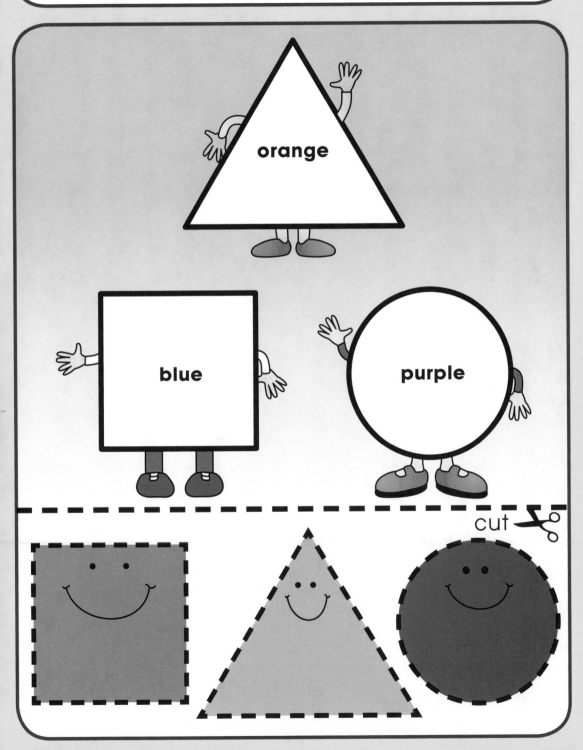

CD-104334

49

Color each space to find the hidden picture.
R = red   G = green   Y = yellow

Color the zebra.

b = black

Color the objects. Draw a line to match each object to the correct color word.

red

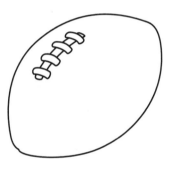

yellow

brown

Circle the two objects in each row that are usually the same color. Color the objects.

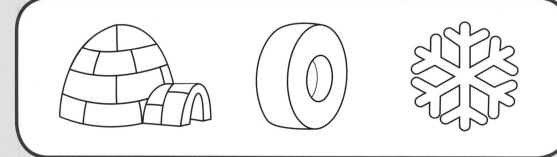

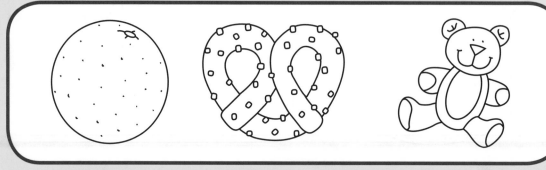

CD-104334

Color the objects. Draw a line to match each object to the correct color word.

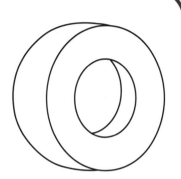

purple

brown

black

Color the flamingos pink.

CD-104334 © Carson-Dellosa

Cut out each shape. Paste it on the shape with the matching color word.

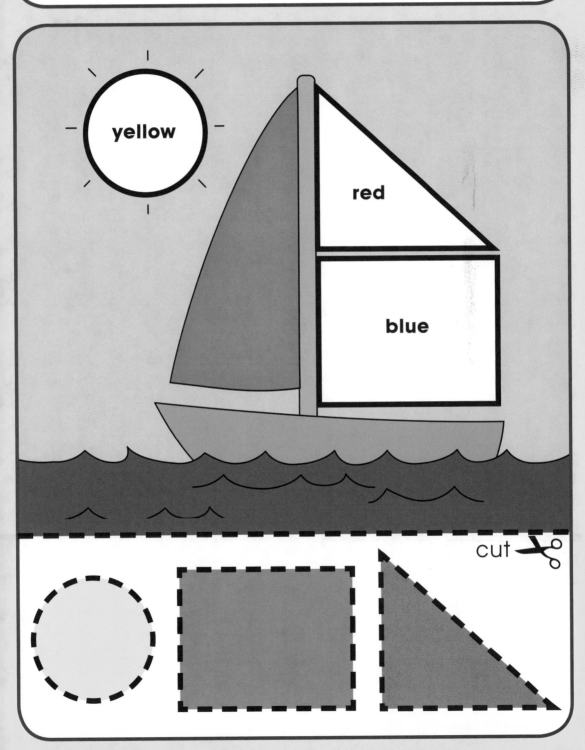

cut

Circle the two objects in each row that are usually the same color. Color the objects.

CD-104334 **59**

Color the objects. Draw a line to match each object to the correct color word.

orange

green

blue

CD-104334

© Carson-Dellosa

Draw a line through the orange objects to help the rabbit find the carrots.

Color the paint cans to match the color words.

red

green

blue

orange

yellow

purple

pink

brown

black

CD-104334

Color the paints to match the color words.

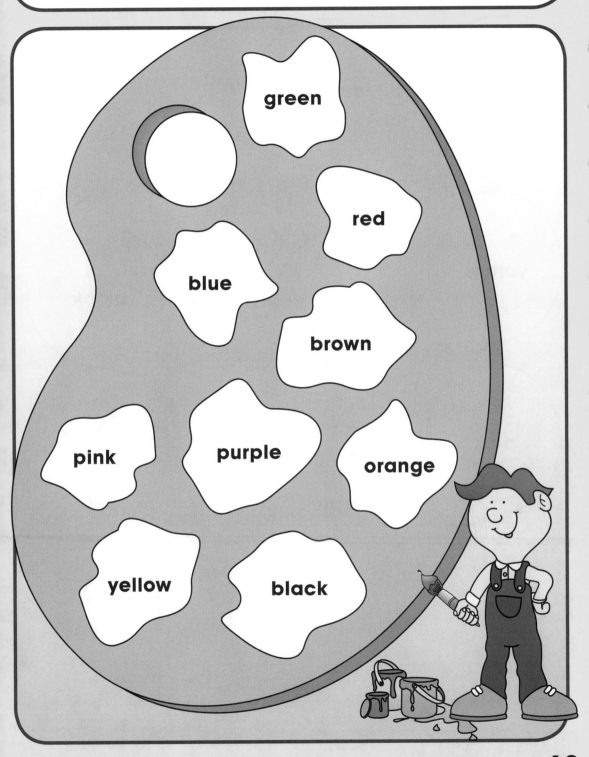

Color the balloons to match the color words.

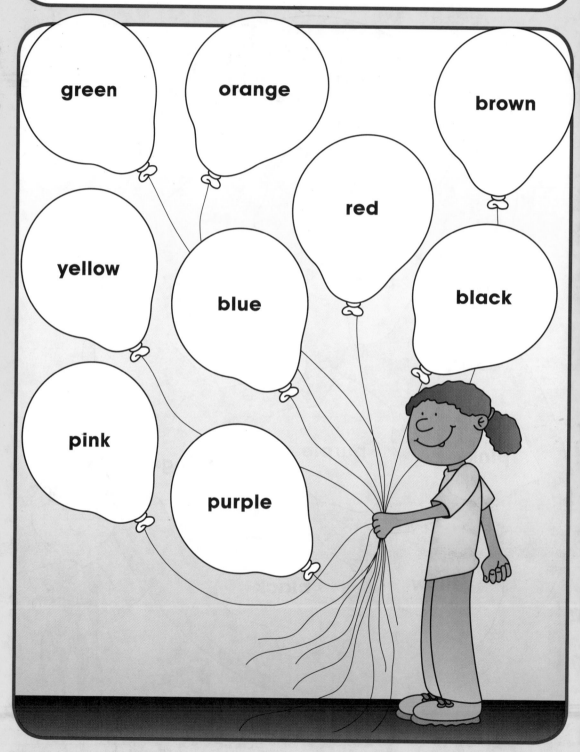

CD-104334